RUSSELL WESTBROOK

Matt Doeden

Lerner Publications ◆ Minneapolis

Lerner Publications Company
A division of Lerner Publishing Group, Inc.
241 First Avenue North
Minneapolis, MN 55401 USA

For reading levels and more information, look up this title at www.lernerbooks.com.

Main body text set in Albany Std 15/22. Typeface provided by Agfa.

Library of Congress Cataloging-in-Publication Data

Names: Doeden, Matt, author.
Title: Russell Westbrook / Matt Doeden.
Description: Minneapolis : Lerner Publications, [2017] | Series: Sports All-Stars |
    Includes bibliographical references and index. | Audience: Ages: 7–11. | Audience:
    Grades: 4 to 6.
Identifiers: LCCN 2016029322 (print) | LCCN 2016030786 (ebook) | ISBN
    9781512425819 (lb : alk. paper) | ISBN 9781512431223 (pb : alk. paper) | ISBN
    9781512428278 (eb pdf)
Subjects: LCSH: Westbrook, Russell, 1988-—Juvenile literature. | Basketball
    players—United States—Biography—Juvenile literature.
Classification: LCC GV884.W44 D64 2017 (print) | LCC GV884.W44 (ebook) | DDC
    796.332092 [B] —dc23

LC record available at https://lccn.loc.gov/2016029322

Manufactured in the United States of America
1-41349-23293-10/3/2016

CONTENTS

TOUGH GUY

Defenders stay close to Russell Westbrook when he has the ball.

Point guard Russell Westbrook was already known as one of the NBA's toughest players. But Oklahoma City Thunder fans didn't know just how tough he could be. He showed everyone on March 4, 2015, when he returned to the court. Just four days earlier, he'd had surgery to repair a broken bone in his face.

Wearing a mask to protect his face, Westbrook was at his best as the Thunder battled the Philadelphia 76ers. He drove toward the basket, bouncing off the defenders who were in his way.

Westbrook hit shots from near the basket and from a long distance. His pinpoint passes set up teammates for easy scores. He even battled for tough **rebounds**.

The game went to overtime with the score tied. With 38 seconds left in overtime, Westbrook made a jump shot to give the Thunder a three-point lead. Then he sank five of six free throws to help seal the

Westbrook usually shoots right-handed, but he can score with his left hand too.

Westbrook pumps his fist in celebration
after sinking another basket
against the 76ers.

victory. Westbrook finished the game with 49 points, 16 rebounds, and 10 assists. It was his fourth straight **triple double**.

"It's amazing watching him play," said Philadelphia's Jason Richardson. "He takes no plays off. He plays hard on both ends of the court. He rebounds. It's amazing to see a guy who has that much passion about winning."

BURSTING ONTO
THE SCENE

In high school, Westbrook wasn't as tall or strong as many top basketball players.

In 2002, Russell Westbrook didn't look like a future NBA star when he enrolled at Leuzinger High School in Lawndale, California. He stood just 5 feet 8 inches (1.7 meters) tall as a freshman. He weighed just 140 pounds (64 kilograms). He wasn't even a starting player for the school's basketball team until he was a junior. "I wasn't that good," Westbrook said. "But I played hard."

Tragedy

One of Westbrook's best friends and high school teammates was Khelcey Barrs. The two friends had hoped to play college basketball together. But one day in 2004, Barrs collapsed after a game. He died from a heart condition.

Westbrook wears a wristband that reads "KB3" to remember his friend. "I feel like I'm playing for him in a way," Westbrook says.

Westbrook often wears two wristbands during games. One reads "KB3," and the other says "Why Not?"

In high school, Westbrook was a star in the classroom as well as on the basketball court. He was offered an academic scholarship to Stanford University. Westbrook's favorite subject was math.

Westbrook hit a growth spurt before his senior year. At 6 feet 3 inches (1.9 m), he bloomed into a star on the court. Westbrook led Leuzinger to a 25–4 record that year. He averaged more than 25 points per game. Suddenly, college **scouts** were noticing him. Westbrook accepted an athletic scholarship to attend UCLA.

During UCLA's 2006–2007 season, Westbrook didn't play much as a freshman. He began the next

Westbrook *(left)* laughs with his UCLA teammates during a game.

season on the bench as well. Then star UCLA guard Darren Collison suffered an injury. Westbrook took Collison's spot on the court.

With more playing time, Westbrook made an instant impact for UCLA. His ballhandling, shooting, and hard-nosed play made him one of the nation's top guards. Westbrook led the team to the **conference** title. He was named the conference Defensive Player of the Year. UCLA went on to the **NCAA Tournament**, where they advanced all the way to the Final Four.

Westbrook soars for a basket. He averaged 12.7 points per game for UCLA in 2007-2008.

Westbrook is able to hit shots from anywhere on the court.

NBA scouts considered Westbrook one of the top **prospects** in the nation. He decided to leave UCLA after his second season to enter the 2008 NBA **Draft**. The Seattle SuperSonics selected him with the fourth overall pick. But Westbrook didn't stay long in Seattle. That summer, the team moved and changed its name. Westbrook would start his NBA career as a member of the Oklahoma City Thunder.

Westbrook smiles for the cameras after being chosen by Seattle in the 2008 NBA Draft.

Westbrook is serious before games, but he has fun during practice.

Westbrook is famous for his on-court intensity. That attitude extends to his time off the court as well. Before a game, he doesn't joke with his teammates. Instead, he sits quietly in the locker room, listening to music and thinking about the game to come. "He doesn't talk," said teammate Anthony Morrow. "He doesn't blink."

Athleticism is a big part of Westbrook's success. But natural talent alone is not enough to star in the NBA. His workout routine includes lots of strength training to tone his muscles. The work pays off. Westbrook is one of the league's strongest guards. That allows him to attack the basket and battle for rebounds, even when surrounded by much bigger players.

Westbrook's strength helps him soar to the basket.

Westbrook's workouts often focus on balance and stability. Because of his fierce style of play, he is always at risk of injury. Working to improve his body control as he flies around the court helps keep him from getting hurt.

Westbrook doesn't rely on a careful diet plan. He tries to maintain good food habits, such as eating smaller portions at mealtime. He also avoids fried foods and eats healthful snacks such as fruit and granola. His favorite pregame meal is a peanut butter and jelly sandwich.

Mental fitness is as important to Westbrook's success as his physical condition. He is highly aggressive, especially when trying to score. The moment the game starts, Westbrook is in attack mode.

Before a game, Westbrook works on controlling his body while he dribbles and runs.

To get his mind ready for a game, he watches video of his opponents. He looks for their strengths and weaknesses so that he knows just how to attack.

Westbrook's mental and physical toughness is legendary. In the 2012–2013 playoffs, he suffered a serious knee injury in the first half of a game. He played the second half anyway. Many

Westbrook uses crutches to walk after injuring his knee in 2013.

believed the injury would force him to miss most of the next season. But he worked all summer to heal the injury and was in the starting lineup for the third game of the 2013–2014 season. He plays when he's hurt, and he doesn't hold back.

WHY NOT?

Westbrook always looks good off the court.

Westbrook has a big personality.

Off the court, he's outspoken, lively, and devoted to family. He calls his parents before every game. He spends time shopping, bowling, playing video games, and learning to play guitar. One thing Westbrook doesn't spend his free time doing is watching basketball. "[I've] got other things to do with my life," he said.

Mr. and Mrs. Westbrook

While at UCLA, Westbrook met Nina Earl. She was a player on UCLA's women's basketball team at the time. The two hit it off. In August 2015, they married. The wedding was held in Beverly Hills, California. Guests included NBA stars Kevin Durant, James Harden, and Kevin Love, as well as many other athletes and celebrities.

Nina Earl and Russell Westbrook

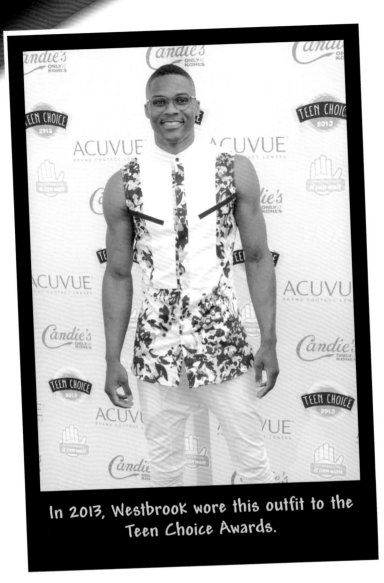

In 2013, Westbrook wore this outfit to the Teen Choice Awards.

Westbrook prides himself on his unique fashion sense. He often wears wild outfits to games and public events. He dresses in bright and sometimes mismatched colors, quirky hats, and unusual eyeglass frames. Westbrook never wears the same thing twice. He wears an outfit once, and then he gives it away.

Westbrook has turned his love of fashion into a business. In 2014, he launched Westbrook Frames eyewear. A short time later, he started his own fashion line called Westbrook XO. He encourages young people to express themselves through fashion. "You can wear anything if you are confident in it," he says.

Helping people is another of Westbrook's passions. He is generous with his time and money. In 2015, he was honored with the NBA Community Assist Award for his charity work.

Westbrook poses with the Community Assist Award in 2015.

In 2012, he started the Russell Westbrook Why Not? Foundation. As a kid, Westbrook's parents taught him to ask, "Why not?" whenever he was told that he couldn't do something. It's a message he passes on to kids. At camps and other events, he tells kids in difficult situations to believe in themselves and ask, "Why not?"

Spending time with kids and helping them reach their dreams is a big part of Westbrook's life.

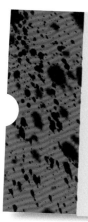

Basketball isn't the only sport Westbrook loves. He also loves to bowl. He hosts a charity bowling event each year. Westbrook says his average bowling score is around 190.

Westbrook bowls at an event for the Russell Westbrook Why Not? Foundation.

In 2015, Westbrook made news by giving a lot of money to his former college, UCLA. It was the largest donation a former basketball player had ever made to the school. The money will help build Russell Westbrook Court, a new practice court for UCLA athletes.

SUPERSTAR GUARD

Westbrook (right) celebrates a basket with Kevin Durant.

Westbrook may have been a late bloomer in high school and college. But that wasn't true in the NBA. He was named to the NBA's All-Rookie Team for the 2008–2009 season. A year later, he and Thunder star Kevin Durant led the team to the playoffs. The duo had quickly made Oklahoma City one of the NBA's most exciting teams.

In 2010–2011, Westbrook was voted to his first All-Star Game. The Thunder returned to the playoffs and reached the Western Conference Finals before losing to the Dallas Mavericks. The next season, Westbrook and his team took another big step. They made it to the NBA Finals, where they lost to the Miami Heat.

Injuries plagued the Thunder over the next few years. Westbrook hurt his knee in the 2013 playoffs. Durant also missed time due to injury. The 2014–2015 season was the biggest disappointment yet for Oklahoma City. The team missed the playoffs. But Westbrook led the NBA with an average of 28.1 points per game.

In 2015–2016, many fans didn't know what to expect from the Thunder. Would they play like one of the best teams in the NBA, as they had two years ago? Or would they repeat the disappointment of 2014–2015? The team started off slowly. But they caught fire in the second half of the season and made the playoffs. Westbrook sank layups and hit jump shots. He dished out assists,

Westbrook soars during the 2011 NBA All-Star Game.

played tough defense, and rebounded the ball. The Thunder crushed Dallas in the first round of the playoffs. Then the Thunder stunned the heavily favored San Antonio Spurs in the second round to win again.

Next up was the Western Conference Finals against the powerful Golden State Warriors. The Warriors were the defending champs. They had just set the all-time regular-season record with 73 wins. Yet Westbrook and the Thunder stormed out to a 3–1 series lead. He helped win Game 4 with a triple double. But the Thunder couldn't close out the Warriors. Golden State won the final three games to end Oklahoma City's season.

The Thunder's future remains a hot topic in the NBA. After the 2015–2016 season, Durant left the team to join Golden State. Will Westbrook be able to carry the Thunder to victory without Durant? One thing is certain. Westbrook remains one of the NBA's fiercest competitors. Basketball fans love his passion for the game and his will to win. With his spirit on the court and his personality off of it, he'll continue to be one of the game's most popular players.

Westbrook greets fans in Oklahoma City.

All-Star Stats

One of the great feats for a basketball player is the triple double. A player must reach double figures in three major statistical categories—usually points, rebounds, and assists—during a game to earn one. In 2015–2016, Westbrook posted 18 of them. Only two players—Oscar Robertson and Wilt Chamberlain—have ever had more triple doubles in a single season.

Most Triple Doubles in a Season in NBA History

41 Oscar Robertson, 1961–1962

31 Wilt Chamberlain, 1973–1974

26 Oscar Robertson, 1960–1961

26 Oscar Robertson, 1963–1964

22 Oscar Robertson, 1964–1965

22 Wilt Chamberlain, 1966–1967

20 Oscar Robertson, 1962–1963

18 Russell Westbrook, 2015–2016

18 Magic Johnson, 1981–1982

Source Notes

7   "Russell Westbrook Hits Career Highs in Points (49), Boards (16) in OT Win," *ESPN*, March 5, 2015, http://espn.go.com/nba/recap?gameId=400579196.

9   Lee Jenkins, "Russell Westbrook Opens Up: All There Really Is to the Thunder Superstar," *Sports Illustrated*, March 31, 2015, http://www.si.com/nba/2015/04/01/russell-westbrook-oklahoma-city-thunder-sports-illustrated.

9   Arash Markazi, "Westbrook: The Honor Guard," *ESPN*, April 30, 2010, http://espn.go.com/los-angeles/nba/columns/story?id=5150492.

15   Jenkins, "Russell Westbrook."

19   Royce Young, "Everything You Always Wanted to Know about Russell Westbrook but Were Afraid to Ask," *ESPN*, May 24, 2016, http://espn.go.com/nba/story/_/id/15628762/everything-always-wanted-know-russell-westbrook-were-afraid-ask.

21   Christina Cauterucci, "Russell Westbrook Is Turning the NBA Playoffs into a Personal Runway Show," *Slate*, May 10, 2016, http://www.slate.com/blogs/xx_factor/2016/05/10/russell_westbrook_is_turning_the_nba_playoffs_into_a_personal_runway_show.html.

Glossary

athleticism: natural strength, speed, and quickness

conference: a group of teams that play against one another

draft: the system by which teams select players entering a league

NCAA Tournament: a yearly tournament held to determine a champion for college basketball's top level

prospects: players who are expected to succeed at the next level of a sport

rebounds: grabbing the ball after missed shots

scholarship: money used to support a student's tuition

scouts: people who judge the skills of players

triple double: reaching a total of 10 or more in three stats categories (usually points, assists, and rebounds in a single game)

Jr. NBA
http://jr.nba.com

Moussavi, Sam. *Oklahoma City Thunder*. New York: AV^2 by
Weigl, 2016.

NBA.com—Russell Westbrook
http://www.nba.com/thunder/team/playerpage_
westbrook_1011.html

Russell Westbrook Why Not? Foundation
http://rwwhynotfoundation.org

Savage, Jeff. *Kevin Durant*. Minneapolis: Lerner Publications,
2012.

Savage, Jeff. *Super Basketball Infographics*. Minneapolis:
Lerner Publications, 2015.

Index

Photo Acknowledgments

The images in this book are used with the permission of: © iStockphoto.com/iconeer (gold and silver stars); Torrey Purvey/Icon Sportswire/Newscom, p. 2; AP Photo/ Sue Ogrocki, pp. 4, 6, 7, 14, 17, 27; © Ken Hively/Los Angeles Times/Getty Images, p. 8; AP Photo/David Zalubowski, p. 9; AP Photo/Michael Conroy, p. 10; AP Photo/ Danny Moloshok, p. 11; AP Photo/Paul Sakuma, p. 12; AP Photo/Julie Jacobson, p. 13; © Paul Moseley/Fort Worth Star-Telegram/Getty Images, p. 15; AP Photo/Rick Bowmer, p. 16; © Michael Stewart/WireImage/Getty Images, p. 18; © Amy & Stuart Photography/Getty Images, p. 19; © Gregg DeGuire/WireImage/Getty Images, p. 20; © Layne Murdoch/NBAE/Getty Images, pp. 21, 23; © Vivien Killilea/Why Not? Foundaton/Getty Images, p. 22; Larry W. Smith/Newscom, p. 24; © Jeff Gross/Getty Images, p. 28.

Front cover: Torrey Purvey/Icon Sportswire/Newscom (Russell Westbrook); © iStockphoto.com/neyro2008 (motion lines); © iStockphoto.com/ulimi (black and white stars); © iStockphoto.com/iconeer (gold and silver stars).